SELECTED POEMS

1943–1966

PHILIP LAMANTIA

A new edition

Edited and with an afterword by Garrett Caples

CITY LIGHTS BOOKS / SAN FRANCISCO

Selected Poems of Philip Lamantia, 1943–1966
Copyright © 1943–1967, 2024 by Nancy J. Peters for the Estate of Philip Lamantia
Afterword copyright © 2024 by Garrett Caples
All Rights Reserved

Book design by Patrick Barber, after the original Pocket Poets edition

Library of Congress Cataloging-in-Publication Data

Names: Lamantia, Philip, 1927–2005, author. | Caples, Garrett T., editor.
Title: Selected poems: 1943–1966 / Philip Lamantia; edited and with an afterword by Garrett Caples.
Description: San Francisco: City Lights Books, 2025. | Series: Pocket Poets; no. 20
Identifiers: LCCN 2024029695 | ISBN 9780872869349 (paperback)
Subjects: LCGFT: Poetry.
Classification: LCC PS3562.A42 A6 2025 | DDC 811/.54—dc23/eng/20240628
LC record available at https://lccn.loc.gov/2024029695

City Lights Books are published at the City Lights Bookstore
261 Columbus Avenue, San Francisco, CA 94133
citylights.com

Contents

REVELATIONS OF A SURREAL YOUTH (1943–1945)   5

TRANCE PORTS (1948–1961)   35

SECRET FREEDOM (1963–1966)   71

AFTERWORD   101
*The Hand Set Free to Dream: The Correspondence of
Philip Lamantia and Lawrence Ferlinghetti*

For the first section of this book, REVELATIONS OF A SURREAL YOUTH, I have chosen poems from the following limited editions of my work: *Erotic Poems* (Bern Porter Books, Berkeley 1946) and from an extensive collection of early poems, *Touch of the Marvelous* (Oyez, Berkeley 1966); second section, TRANCE PORTS, is selected from *Ekstasis* (1959) and *Destroyed Works* (1962), both published by Auerhahn Press, San Francisco; one poem originally appeared in the magazine, *El Como Emplumado*. The third section, SECRET FREEDOM, *is published here for the first time anywhere.*

P. L.

Revelations of a Surreal Youth

THERE ARE MANY PATHWAYS
TO THE GARDEN

If you are bound for the sun's empty plum
there is no need to mock the wine tongue
but if you are going to a rage of pennies
over a stevedore's wax ocean
then, remember: all long pajamas are frozen dust
unless an axe cuts my flaming grotto.

You are one for colonial lizards
and over bathhouses of your ear
skulls shall whisper
of a love for a crab's rude whip
and the rimless island of refusal shall seat itself
beside the corpse of a dog
that always beats a hurricane
in the mad run for Apollo's boxing glove.

As your fingers melt a desert
an attempt is made to marry the lily-and-fig-foot dragon
mermaids wander and play with a living cross
a child invents a sublime bucket of eyes
and I set free the dawn of your desires.

The crash of your heart
beating its way through a fever of fish
is heard in every crowd of that thirsty tomorrow
and your trip ends in the mask of my candle-lit hair.

THE TOUCH OF THE MARVELOUS

The mermaids have come to the desert
They are setting up a boudoir next to the camel
who lies at their feet of roses

A wall of alabaster is drawn over their heads
by four rainbow men
whose naked figures give off a light
that slowly wriggles upon the sands

I am touched by the marvelous
as the mermaids' nimble
fingers go through my hair
that has come down forever from my head
to cover my body:
a savage fruit of lunacy

Behold, the boudoir is flying away
and I am holding onto the leg of the lovely one
called beneath the sea
BIANCA
She is turning
with the charm of a bird
into two giant lips
and I am now falling into the goblet of suicide

She is the angelic doll turned black
she is the child of broken elevators
she is the curtain of holes
you never want to throw away
she is the first woman and the first man
and I am lost to have her

I am hungry for the secrets of the sadistic fish
I am plunging into the sea

I am looking for the region
where the smoke of your hair is thick
where you are again climbing over the white wall
where your eardrums play music
to the cat that crawls in my eyes
I am recalling memories of you BIANCA

I am looking beyond the hour and the day
to find you BIANCA

PLUMAGE OF RECOGNITION

A soul drenched in the milk of marble
goes through the floor of an evening
that rides lost on a naked virgin
It gains power over the dull man:
it is a soul sucked by lepers

What liquid hour shall rivet
its song on my cat
with the neck of all space ?

Morning and I may lose
the terrible coat of ill feeling
that has curled me into a chained dragon
the flower bursting with eyelids

Ah a fever the skeleton of arson!
comes to rest on the citadel of the immortals;
the diadem flickers and dies away
while running toward the vat of salted babies

They are creeping upon the wall my dagger
they are bulging with cradles
the era of the lunatic birds has arrived!

They have come to rape the town
infested with iron-blood clerks
and to send the hairless priests
to the pool of deadly anchors

Parades are the enchantment of a brain
piled-up like the water of an ocean
I enjoy the creation of a human table
to be in the center of the delirious crowd

There are birds perched on my bones
that will soon flood the avenues
with their serpent-like feathers
I am at a house built by Gaudi
"May I come in ?"

HERMETIC BIRD

This sky is to be opened
this plundered body to be loved
this lantern to be tied
around the fangs of your heart

Lost on a bridge
going across oceans of tragedy
across islands of inflammable women
I stand

with my feathers entangled in your navel
with my wings opalescent in the night
and shout words heard tomorrow
in a little peasant cart
of the seventeenth century

Breath by breath
the vase in the tomb
breaks to give birth to a roving Sphinx
Tremble, sweet bird, sweet lion
hunger for you
hunger for your mother

The children in the lamps
play with our hair
swinging over the void

Here is a landscape on fire
Here are horses wet by the sour fluids of women

On the pillars of nicotine
the word *pleasure* is erased by a dog's tongue
On the pillars the bodies are opened by keys
the keys are nailed to my bed
to be touched at dawn
to be used in a dream

If one more sound is heard
the children will come to murder
at the bottom of the lake
at the bottom of the lake

If the children murder
the owls will bleed
the wanton humans
who parade in basements of the sun

When the columns fall into the sea
with a crash involving prophecies and madmen
together in a little cradle
lifted into the robes of desire
and with our mouths opened for the stars
howling for the castles to melt at our feet
you and I
will ride over the breasts of our mother
who knows no one
who was born from unknown birds
forever in silence
forever in dreams
forever in the sweat of fire

YOU AND I HAVE NOTHING TO FEAR

Listen
you may hear the ten may poles
out of a womb
pulled through the child's stupefying algebra
of sound
but only if you dip bracelets
in your blood
scratch out the eyes set in my ruby
that is
in turn
set in the sun
washed and preserved
for the rays of urine

>   There are more invisibilities
>   to be attained

Heavy as the convulsive murderers
hanged at midnight
—somewhere north of our pathways—
swinging over cold islands
in the bowels of the city
As heavy as I have said
you appear with a diamond hatchet
floating over our bodies
whose toads bathe in the eloquent lakes
that no one will ever see again
whose radiant blue columns
spit sperm over the city

On the dogs whispers pop-off
to become songs in the sky
infested with elegance
an elegance which no one has the right to understand
just as no one has the right to understand
why you were bom in a house of cigarettes
or I in a howling star

But hold your basket of berries
don't let them fall into the sky-rocketing bones
You may regret having these little cards
with the numbers written over them
but you'll want to hold them close to you
when the flowers come back to the mummies

Rest In Peace
Over the night these words scatter themselves
And as I say this
bloodless nuns pass with lanterns
in their withering hands
They shall kneel until mid-day
forms a dagger for their hearts

Rest assured
we have not been uttering a word
against the master
His leafy ears heal too quickly
and besides the stars have crossed over
our tight embrace
You and I have nothing to fear
not even the bloody sunrise
as it invades the fog
lifting the turbulent aura to our faces

AUTOMATIC WORLD

The sun has drowned
virgins are no more
there is no need for understanding
but there is so much to see

So come with me
down the boulevard
of crawling veins
Don't be afraid
blood is cheap!

A paradise song ?
A dirty story?
A love sonnet?
Scream it out!
Then we'll have the human walls
tumbling down to meet our march
into the raw-meat city!

The velvet robes are strewn
across the landscape
We step upon the sidewalk
that goes up and down
up to the clouds
down to the starving people
Don't ask me what to do!
Keep on going
we'll end up somewhere fast
on the moon perhaps!

Rainbow guns are dancing
in front of the movie queens
Everyone is laughing
flying dying
never knowing when to rest
never knowing when to eat

And the fountains come falling
out of her thistle-covered breasts
and the dogs are happy
and the clowns are knifing
and the ballerinas are eating stone

O the mirror-like dirt
of freshly spilt blood
trickling down the walls
the walls that reach the stars!

O the flock of sheep
breaking their flesh open
with bones sucked
from the brothels!

O the grave of bats
sailing through shops
with the violent hands!

When will these come ?
When will these go ?

The sun is riding into your eye
virgins are bursting
from under my flaming palms
and we are slowly floating away

THE ISLANDS OF AFRICA

to Rimbaud

Two pages to a grape fable
dangles the swan of samite blood
shaping sand from thistle covered fog
Over sacred lakes of fever
(polished mouths of the vegetable frog
rolling to my iron venus)
I drop the chiseled pear
Standing in smoke filled valleys
(great domains of wingless flight
and the angel's fleshy gun)
I stamp the houses of withering wax
Bells of siren-teeth (singing to our tomb
refusal's last becoming)
await the approach of the incendiary children
lighting the moon-shaped beast

Every twisted river pulls down my torn-out hair
to ratless columns by the pyramid's ghost
(watered basin of the temple stink)
and all the mud clocks in haste
draw their mermaid-feather swords
(wrapped by Dust) to nail them
into the tears of the sea-gull child
The winter web minute
flutters beneath the spider's goblet
and the whores of all the fathers
bleed for my delight

A WINTER DAY

In the rose creeping into the tower of exiles
when the buffet is laden with jewels
when the night is filled with hate
when the womb of Eros is deserted
when the sleeping men are awakened
when the old lovers are no longer frightened
—my heart

The old women come down playing on the lawns
of the intangible murderers
the women are mine
Your eye is so smooth in the sunlight
you are no longer a child
you are old
spider of the blind
insolent mother
Do you care for my young hair
I want to lay the fibres of my heart over your face

It is a strange moment
as we tear ourselves apart in the silence
of this landscape
of this whole world
that seems to go beyond its own existence

You roll so beautifully over my bones
that have shaken off the flesh of their youth
My nakedness is never alarming
it is this way I adore you

Your hands with crystals shining into the night
pass through my blood
and sever the hands of my eyes

We have come to a place where the nightingales sleep
We are filling the oceans and plains
with the old images of our phosphorescent bones

A CIVIL WORLD

In a moment their faces will be visible.

You shall see the women who walk in a night of offensive sunlight that cuts through their cardboard thighs.

As the street is cleaned by the presidents of the nation, I can see the bowlegged men moving over to copulate with the maniacs.

As a rose runs down an alley, a purple nugget, giving off some blood, is suspended in air.

The children who are ten feet tall are wet.

Their faces are scorched, their eyes cut by glass.

They play their games as a steeple topples, as a clown's laugh is heard in church.

Quietly the mothers are killing their sons; quietly the fathers are raping their daughters.

But the women.

The eye wanders to a garden in the middle of the street.

There are poets dipping their diamond-like heads in the luminous fountain. There are grandmothers playing with the delicate toys of the chimera. There are perfumes being spilt on the garbage. There is a drunken nun flying out of a brothel.

The women are all colors.

Their breasts open like flowers, their flesh spreads over the park like a blanket. Their hair is soaked in the blood of their lovers, those who are the mirrors of this night.

The naked lovers! All of them, fifteen years old! One can still see their hair growing! They come from the mountains, from the stars even, with their handsome eyes of stone. Ah, these somnambulistic lovers, with their bellies full of arrows!

After the street has recaptured its loneliness, a precious stone casts its light on the perambulator I am to enter. One perambulator in the center of a world. A poet—far way in the mountains—can be heard chanting like an ape. I wonder when he will stop?

THE ENORMOUS WINDOW

Within closets filled with nebulae
the blood shot eyes
swim upward for the sun

This world of serpents and weeping women
is crushed in the violence
of a swamp large enough to contain
the enormous razorblade of the night

>   *In the tropics*
>   *the doctors prescribe*
>   *sand for the heart*

>   *Ad astra*
>   *Ad astra*

With fire spitting across the horizon
and like a little flake of flesh
bashed against our heads
midnight seeps through the marigolds
in the garden no longer quiet
as corpses float through its arbor of palm trees

Neurosthenics
with young blood
ride to the stars
with horses from Peru

>   *Tomorrow evangelists*
>   *the following day toys fall in love*

the last moment brings rabid boys
beating their fathers with lightning rods—

Ad Astra
Ad Astra

In the sea the clown of windows
encounters swift rocks
climbing upon his body
to rub against his wooden anus

As the jungle disappears
one theater of war gives birth to another
The bleeding eyes of murder
fall into the sea of this night

The performance begins
in the palm of your hand
where the swords mark the spot
where your eardrums take wings
to gather strength between two girls
raped at sunrise

Through the ceiling I can see beggars
walking on hands and knees
to reach a pyramid flung into the storm
where serpents drink champagne
and wash their women with the blood of prophets
The stars are wet tonight
the naked schoolmasters
are no longer in the gardens of childhood
and the sea has been heated for lions

And now you can bleed fire from statues
and die lower you descend into this bottomless pit
the higher will you rise
beyond the raped girls
beyond the wounded boys
trapped in the labyrinth
of their mother's hair
    beyond the soiled curtain of space

AWAKENED FROM SLEEP

Swept from the clouds
we are among gardens under the sea.
Flaming white windows
from which nightingales flaunt in the sun.

Have we come from the cities of the plain
or the moon's lake of demons?

Your whole body is a wing,
daughter of half-seen worlds;
together we fly to rocks of flesh
beneath the ashes of ancient lovers.

There is no rule here,
no seasons and no misery;
there are only our desires
revealed in the mist.
Here ghosts are reborn every moment
in the spider webs of your face.

Your hair is mingled with little children
laughing in the moonlight;
butterflies have come to rest upon your lips
whose words clothe the dancing stars
falling lightly to earth.
You have become so monumental,
and I so sleepy.
Water is trickling down your lucid breasts.
In a minute you'll be a shadow
and I a flame in sleep.

We'll meet,
corridors will open,
the rain will come in,
the hot bite of dogs will be upon us.
And drifting with a marvelous touch
of all the moons of space,
    will be the lovers,
diffusing their blood
in the secret passageways of the heart.

MIRROR AND HEART

The teacups shattered upon the legs of ancient lovers
become a statue in Rome before you
my embittered gypsy

Pluck your feathers
stain the wings that carry your heart among assassins
Watch through the boudoir the satin shirts of drunken men
who have seen their poisoned hair scattered in fire
watch and regret nothing

Your fate is to follow the sleeping women
in the castle of memory with its smoked oceanic rocks
covered by blood and snow

Your body reclaiming the stars
lifts itself in a wooden frame
to be seen in boulevards
that twist themselves at dawn into my room

Advance with caution
as with locust in your belly
make a window that will follow the trees into a lake

Each bridegroom shall inherit a laugh of childhood
that will announce the coming of my felons
soft with murder
soft with your feathers growing upon their hands

The noiseless girl who places the eyes of her lover
in a glass of wine
is only a flower set between the oars of a boat
to petrify and to be sucked for blood

Don't be frightened my dark one
this dream that winds its way
against a mask worn by the first suicide
will fade away into another's fury
when the morning wears your torn dress

Awakened at the side of this hunted slave
your hands will whisper my name into the sands

As your lips raise water from the mist
an apparition of your mirror
takes you within its warmth
reflecting black wounds set open by the fingernail of the dumb

Solitude is your violence

Your burnt face is fading into the dream

My love
my gypsy
among the fallen you are luminous
You wander with those who are mystery
with a naked heart upon your breast

THE DIABOLIC CONDITION

As the women who live within each other's bodies
descend from their polar regions
to the circle of demons
I become ready to offer myself to the smooth red snakes
    entwined in the heads of sorcerers

Between the black arms coming over the swamp
rushing to embrace me
and the distant sun in which abide the men who hold
    within their fists the Evil Eyes
between the tombs and beds of boneless magicians
who have worked in the secrecy of abandoned towers
despite my body flying away
despite the lizards who crawl into the altars where
    the potents are being prepared
despite the intrusion of doctor's maids
    and egyptologists
despite the old Doric temple carried in by the art lovers
despite the nest of mad beggars
the chant is heard
and the words of the chant are written in oceanic gardens

The flat walls are singing good-bye
we have entered the city where the dead masters speak to us
    of catacombs and the horned enchantress of Africa
The incantation is following us into the streets
and into the sky
We are ascending to the limitless cosmos of architecture
we are crawling backward to enormous hearts
that leap over the snow to climb into our bodies

Come my ritual wax and circles
my rose spitting blood
When the day is lit up by our magic candles
and the hours yell their sadistic songs and suck hard
into the night when the cats invade our skulls
then we will know the destructive ones have gone
out into the world to watch the cataclysm begin
as the final wave of fire pours out from their hearts

THE IMAGE OF ARDOR

for Parker Tyler

In the tropical islands
that cut through hearts,
beasts, ogres,—the wounded children
separate, become machines of wonder,
follow their thorned fathers
whose mouths contain lakes,
sweet scented cascades,
murdered girls with the eyes of zebras;
follow them to the lamps of flesh
that burn through our diamonds
that draw sweat from the trees of blue iron.

The heavy submarine women
pass over the bodies of wanton youths
who search for ravens lost in swamps,
who roll their eyes in heated bottles,
pursue their lovers with flaming torches
and carry their priceless mirrors
within a network of navel strings.

These painted faces watch only the incomparable,
love only the unopposed flowers of desire.
The lions that issue from lava
claim them, embrace their naked bodies.
They live within wild birds
swiftly ascending mountains of flame.
Their pride is kept within a perfumed box
that sails in a sea of hair,
to land on this island

and be sold to many men
who dwell beneath heated jewels,
beneath the secret idols of love.

Hidden in rocks, in grass of blood,
the youth has grown enormous wings.
He dreams of black chimeras
and wonders about the huge pair of breasts
that sink into the sea.

I AM COMING

I am following her to the wavering moon
to a bridge by the long waterfront
to valleys of beautiful arson
to flowers dead in a mirror of love
to meii eating wild minutes from a clock
to hands playing in celestial pockets
and to that dark room beside a castle
of youthful voices singing to the moon.

When the sun comes up she will live at a sky
covered with sparrow's blood
and wrapped in robes of lost decay.

But I am coming to the moon,
and she will be there in a musical night,
in a night of burning laughter
burning like a road of my brain
pouring its arm into the lunar lake.

Trance Ports

INTERSECTION

1

No longer scouring mangoed islands
no longer doves flown from my fingers
no longer the first wave
                rainbowed
over the white stone
             flinging
light to the black reef

No longer the razor from a sheath of stars
    over the face of day
come back from night
                no longer
nautical sleep to float me by the blood cry of doves
on miasma, the sight of crime envelopes day
under cover of love

2

An old look follows me thru the town
a look of daggers and autumn winds
a look that betrays where it came from in a pool
                at my feet
fish comb water and change it into fire

It's useless to ask who's behind these eyes
set like stars in snow
or name the creatures coming alive
        out of the exploding iris
A supper of iron and mercury

is spread out on a table of green water
and the knives, forks and spoons devour it!

I follow the lights of a swayed bridge
and that old look's thrown up from the bay
      at the sputter of dawn
Night does not come, held back
by pins and needles spilt from the sun
—and old look of ties undone,
of lambs martyred by the will of the innocent—

This look on the uncrossable bridge—
an eye closes on a rough surface—
if it had power I'd demand atonement
if it spoke I'd speak back
if it were a body I'd wrestle with it!

3

I'm thinking then
a chain of words
breaking at the fistfall of words
I'm thinking green funnels of light
sifting white water
flown in blue
that cut a breast of honey to free the air

Here
take my breath
out of all the cities I haven't seen
from quick pleasures I haven't noticed
from a room without doors I wouldn't want to leave
Take my breath for your breath

In a secret room I dream
    the eye of the father closing
    the eye of the mother closing
the eye of the daughter
              opened

They look to the winter sun
that lifted a golden reef into the clouds

I'm thinking some impossible drug
flown by a hand not a hand
    but a tongue
not a tongue
    but a whip
not a whip but a cup!
I'm thinking
going down the street
too long to be seen
not wide enough to be missed

my house in the cracks of the pavement!

INSIDE THE JOURNEY

Quickly, I rocked between waves. Quickly, I got the god on the wing. Quickly, I picked the tarn from the twirling top. Quickly and quickly, and faster, faster: for the kill of the body's anger, for the win of the lost child, for the fall of wizards through revolving sheets of snow.

And so I walked all the streets become one street among the renegades who go unmolested, half-asleep, to the gardens of childhood—in the largess of a white love once a pink, pearl-shaped object on the horizon of their longing; a white love in a black space—no time in the land of nothing but time.

And this was my dream that lasted from some dawn to some midnight in the falling down room overlooking the oldest graveyard of Manhattan:

> the poisonous stars: *benign*
> the rootless tree: *nailed to the sky*
> the black pit: *enclosing ladders of white light*
> the icebergs of the mind: *floating to the tropics* . . .

For a long time I saw no other sky than the ceiling of this room where, from a chink of plaster, hung the image of paradise I embarked for like a ship to the Orient. I could hardly move my head. I could hardly say the word to ask for water. I could hardly conceive of *another* life. I threw the hex down, I swallowed the spells, I put the tumult down. If I spoke I would violate the wonder of that silence. If I moved, I would break across space like a knife cutting cheese. I knew all the constellations of infinite duration where my thoughts that flew away one day waited like brides for their bridegrooms of the infinite.

In another time, I was making blueprints for the Eternal, but the work was interrupted by some ogre who jumped out from behind a slab of magenta sky, and I was mesmerized on the spot between the poison I was wiping from my lips and the face behind the face I saw looking at me from the sky I was using as a mirror.

Anyway, I broke the spell. But another wave of invented emotions sank and another light fell on the crest of the wave: escape was a door I kept shutting all around me AND on those who were carving me, symbolically they said, for the first course at the restaurant for the initiates of the lake of love—which is to say, sperm ran high that year, breaking over the brains of those who know how to conduct themselves properly in *this* world: which is to say, life goes on gathering wool for the mothers of all the daughters whose tongues spit live lobsters and whose insatiable desire for some seasalt paradise makes thunder break in my skull: which is to say, very simply and without metaphor, that my brain was oppressing me.

—And that is not the most of it—for I took a look into the great vacuum of *this* world, in order that the journey in space of that life that puts poetry to shame, since it strained at the risk of all my senses becoming nil and hurtled me further into abysmal giddiness, would terminate at the junction where I might be able to move while in a state of suspended animation, since if I did not move in the vacuum the vacuum would move within me. And this movement of what is lusting to annihilate the sense of life (instigating panic in the mind, heart and liver) and taking its place, therefore, within life itself—would only lead to my ejection from *this* world.

It is this Vacuum that makes possible that daily hell kept going to decimate the scapegoat inhabitants of the earth, inspiring nothing but apathy and further pollution, revolving on the sexual hydra—at one pole—and fed through the swine mongering mobs at the other pole, in order to do away with the memory of what WAS or MIGHT BE—and as I opened to IT I saw its Body that is a vast machinery, in perpetual motion, for the sole consumption of a certain kind of etherealized excrement transmuted out of the bestial layers of the human condition become entirely the cretinized image of God with whom, be it added, this machine copulates perpetually . . .

ANIMAL SNARED IN HIS REVERY

He breathes through his wounds.
The herbs that would heal him decay in the labyrinth of his great paw.
The sun sends medicinal currents to the wobbling island under his sunken tooth.
With agates of rain, the sibylline garden (oracles speak from the flowers) conceives grimly poisonous minerals traveling the earth veins.
The animal, blackening the light with an orb of his blood, reads on the televised leaves:
—SLEEP TERRORS RAGING—
—EXIT FROM DREAMS—
. . . and the green mouth cracks open underground.

THE OWL

I hear him, see him—interpenetrate
those shadows warping the garden pathways,
as the dark steps I climb are lit up
by his Eye magnetic to the moon,
his Eye magnetic to the moon.

I have not seen him when windows are mute
to whisper his name; on that moment
erroneous bats slip out through the sky.
His lair conceives my heart,
all hearts make the triangle he uses for a nose,
sniffing bloodways to my brain:
the bloodways are lit up by his Eye.

On a sudden appearance he tortures leaves,
flays branches and divides segments
the sun has drawn. I do not falter
in the dark he fortifies.
His color is *green* green,
to distend him over the earth.
He does not fly.
You meet him while walking.

He is not easily enticed to manifestation,
but stony silence, petrified moments
a transfiguration—will bring him out,
focused on the screen where all transfigured bodies are.
You must be humble to his fangs
that paw the moonball dissolving in the space
from the corner of your eye:
he will trick you otherwise
into daylight, where you meet his double while running.

By night, the deltas of the moon-spilled planet
are stoned under his wriggling light.

By day, he chokes the sun.

What made tarot cards and fleurs de lis

What made tarot cards and fleurs de lis
    chariots my heart to shackled towers
The priestess maps apocalypses
    Swords catch on medused hair
        Mandolins woman in a garden

They scaled the wall, they fell from a wall
Fleurs de lis illuminated on an eyeball
    came out of the wall

    they fought in a flower.

Symbologies systematized from sweat suctionings
made theatrical cruelty extend souls on a pensive
cloud turn   turning incendiary incentives ON!

        They came to PEACE
and wailed in gavottes
    monsters cooled their mothers
in bubbling craters
                angels
  dropt leprous booty
On a high flung season they blackened blood,
                            climbing the walls

A fleur de lis on a charging horse swam up
    into the moonclad Knight
his lady on a wall
             raped
                      moon struck by wands
clapt in a bell, his lady shook fleurs de lis on the wind

                    Mandolins
        in a bile styled peace
                         explode!
     Knights go scattering swords
The Tripled Queen on a resinous wall
                              apparitioned
as fleurs de lis
             luminescent
         under burnt out flesh
suddenly galed
                    TAROTED
on medieval   stained   glass

Man is in pain

Man is in pain
    ten bright balls bat the air
    falling through the window
    on which his double leans a net the air made
    to catch the ten bright balls

Man is a room
    where the malefic hand turns a knob
    on the unseen unknown double's door

Man is in pain
    with his navel hook caught on a stone quarry
    where ten bright balls chose to land
    AND where the malefic hand carves
        on gelatinous air THE WINDOW
    to slam shut on his shadow's tail

    Ten bright balls bounce into the unseen
    unknown double's net
Man is a false window
    through which his double walks to the truth
    that falls as ten bright balls
    the malefic hand tossed into the air

Man is in pain
    ten bright spikes nailed to the door!

TERROR CONDUCTION

The menacing machine turns on and off

Across the distance light unflickers active infinities

Under the jangling hand set going in the brain
        THE WOMAN
menacing by white lacerations
   THE MAN
menacing
in a timeweighed fishbowl of the vertical act
and the woman and the man menacing together
        out of mutual crucifixions
disgorge
   towers for the dead

     the woman menacing
the man menacing
the woman and the man menacing together
    BUT
THE CROWDS
   THE CROWDS MENACING
as eyes take off for NOTHINGNESS
in night rememorizing the primal menace
on a day in a night crossed with butchering
polite squeels humdrum
        WHAT are all these
  waywardlooking scorching haggard
       grim
perilous witchlike   criminal
      SUBLIME

```
drunken        wintered
                    GRAZING
       FACES
                 FACES
                           going by
like icebergs
         like music
                  like boats
                           like mechanical toys
LIKE
    RAINING
             SWORDS!
```

PUT DOWN

    of the whore of Babylon

High voltage mires got into her jaw
as she devoutly lit up her spine in front of Mammon

On the slopes of the Sierra Madre de Chihuahua
they dance night fires
cross themselves by mirrors
blood shot emaciated men who—they themselves tell us
        FELL FROM HEAVEN!
dance—light fires—eat bitter earth fruit
in a sense like manna—O man! O man!—
    the spit of plant lice
    or black markets in a pearl at the unheard sound
For the wails of self-pity
    for the hysterical salesmen of ideas
        for the goodwilled destroyers of words
THESE
must be PUT DOWN
                for they're inside us
and foment saccharine sweet whores
like this ONE
Dancing
to the tune of sly poisonous health remedies
    that make my head exude dung!
    that put saliva in my bones!
    that dish out infinite possibility of the
        imago-magpie of erotic ecstasies!
    NO!
        NO!
            NO!

not for this panic of idols coning our time
                              by false angelclocks
but for the descended dove we make it to live!

As some light fell

As some light fell
on the inscaped facade
  stains of interior cancer
        intervined the stars

     bewitched by time, a long room
of rooms who opened on you
                I
                R
                I
                S
the street corner flew into Spring
    ,precisely a lily or an iris—

DEAD SMOKE

Ambivalent miles, sorceries played, we drank from hatred's lake
Giant jades immanated spells, I played the windows of Hell
Perfumed birds out of emblematic halls
cut fire in two—caves yawned walls, cries, tigers
a mile below Saturn
presence of damnation
Shades in the meadow enlightened the cows
who made the walk of seas go round
and legends, iron stalks in the forest, carved the geometries of
                                                                     Azoth

Winds have not flown longer than time we stopped
whose sail hit the rooms where you looked into voids
—a beast on a star, Jaiba on the moon, the sunken tooth—
Stalks of madness tripled fire
and sent gardens under the sea
mountains fell   dogs howled
You—O dark side of the moon—
interlaced light—shadows went on the water—
undeciphered glyphs, stones of the immortals,—trophies bled in
                                                                      gold!

MORNING LIGHT SONG

RED DAWN clouds coming up! the heavens proclaim you, Absolute God
I claim the glory, in you, of singing to you this morning
For I am coming out of myself and Go to you, Lord of the Morning Light
For what's a singer worth if he can't talk to you, My God of Light?
These lines should grow like trees to tie around yr Crown of the Sky
These words should be strong like those of the ancient makers,
O poet of poets
Ancient deity of the poem—
Here's spindle tongue of morning riding the flushes of NIGHT
Here's gigantic ode of the sky about to turn on the fruits of my lyre
Here's Welcome Cry from heart of the womb of words,—Hail, Queen of Night!
Who giveth birth to the Morning Star, Here's the quiet cry of stars broken among crockery
Here's the spoon of sudden birds wheeling the rains of Zeus
Here's the worshipping Eye of my soul stinging the heavens
Here's Charmed Bird, zepher of High Crags—jugs of the divine poem
As it weaves terrestial spaces, overturning tombs, breaking hymens
From where cometh this first cry
that my hands go into for the wresting of words
Here's my chant to you, Morning of Mornings, God of gods, light of light
Here's your singer let loose into the sky of your heaven

For we have come howling and screaming and wailing and I come
    SINGING
To You who giveth forth the song of songs that I am reborn
    from its opulence
That I hold converse with your fantasy That I am your beauty
NOT OF THIS WORLD and bring to nothing all that would
    stop me
From flying straight to your heart whose rays conduct me to the
    SONG!

THE WHEEL

At halls of Oedipus blind
    at interior cairn at Garnac
        at jaguar court of the Quiche flue
I came with Saint-Germain
  washed the feet of lepers dried the tears of widows
  walked a long way to the desert meditated birds
  went the way of wandering anchorite
    chewed the bread of hawks
      looped the dream of Constantine
      was Bishop of Alchemia
        made signs for the people that they knew the Christ
        opened gates of Saint Bruno
          sat still in cave of Saint Druida
          spoke out against the rule of iron!

I came with banquet of lovers at ruins of Tenochtitlan
  swam the Hellespont of antique mystery
    landed on shores of Mu Atlantis Babylon
      made fast for pool of the underworld and
        ascended feet high into the sky--at rigalu of Tingis
        ate from tables of undersea gardens

I came in company of the unknown saint
  prayed to Notre Dame in women's cabinets
    entered hermitages of Basil talked desert tongues
      was desperate in the medieval night
      designed crests for the Due D'Ys
        brought battle on the anglosaxon world.

   Soul in the night
    make the wearer rise with Thee
   to drink with Thee the wines of paradise!
I came with Thee, anointed One, into mechano hells at
 desecrations of the Lily and said
No more this door/ for Love turns in happy feet of fat light we
 watch with eagle eyes
in time and out of time—for Thee!

The night is a space of white marble

The night is a space of white marble
This is Mexico
I'm sitting here, slanted light fixture, pot, altitudinous silence
your voice, Dionysius, telling of darkness, superessential light
In the silence of holy darkness I'm eating a tomato
I'm weak from the altitude
something made my clogged head move!
Rutman a week at beach at Acapulco
Carol Francesca waiting till Christmas heroin rain on them!
I see New York upside down
your head, Charlie Chaplin—in a sling
it's all in the courts of war
                                  sign here—the slip of dung
technically we are all dead
this is my own thought! a hail of hell!
Saint Dionysius reminds us of flight to unknowable Knowledge
the doctrine of initiates completes the meditation!

There is this distance between me and what I see

There is this distance between me and what I see
everywhere immanence of the presence of God
no more ekstasis
a cool head
watch watch watch
I'm here
He's over there . . . It's an Ocean . . .
sometimes I can't think of it, I fail, fall
There IS this look of love
there IS the tower of David
there IS the throne of Wisdom
there IS this silent look of love
Constant flight in air of the Holy Ghost
I long for the luminous darkness of God
I long for the superessential light of this darkness
another darkness I long for the end of longing
I long for the
                it is Nameless what I long for
a spoken word caught in its own meat saying nothing
This nothing ravishes beyond ravishing
There IS this look of love Throne Silent look of love

I have given fair warning

I have given fair warning
Chicago New York Los Angeles have gone down
I have gone to Swan City where the ghost of Maldoror may still roam
The south is very civilized
I have eaten rhinoceros tail
It is the last night among crocodiles
Albion opens his fist in a palm grove
I shall watch speckled jewel grow on the back of warspilt horses
Exultation rides by
A poppy size of the sun in my skull
I have given fair warning
at the time of corpses and clouds I can make love here as anywhere

HIGH

O beato solitudo! where have I flown to?
stars overturn the wall of my music
as flight of birds, they go by, the spirits
opened below the lark of plenty
ovens of neant overflow the docks at Veracruz
This much is time
summer coils the soft suck of night
lone unseen eagles crash thru mud
am worn like an old sack by the celestial bum
I'm dropping my eyes where all the trees turn on fire!
I'm mad to go to you, Solitude—who will carry me there?
I'm wedged in this collision of planets/Tough!
I'm ONGED!
I'm the trumpet of King David
the sinister elevator tore itself limb by limb

>You can not close
>you can not open
>you break yr head
>you make bloody bread!

RESURRECTIONS

1

It is I who create the world and put it to rest
you will never understand me
I have willed your destruction

It's the beginning of the flower
inside it's black ore I salute abyss after abyss

You are the exploding rose of my eyes I have nothing but third
    eyes!

This is the end of clockwork sempitemity is the rose of time

This flower talk will get you nowhere

I will not be involved with people I call true distance
I invite you only to the door of horror
Laughter
I keep stoning you with black stars

> Christ is superior to Apollo
> boddhisatvas are drunk with being God
> he who is living lives only the living live
> I will hate and love in the Way
>   in *this* is Being

I will return to the poem

2

>A theater of masked actors in a trance
>according to the virtues of sacred plants

There are those dying of hunger
mankind is sanctioned crime
men should not die of hunger

It is food, imperialist dogs! FOOD! not culture!

There will come Judgement swift and terrible
war

my actor will say in mask of sick dying poor man
        I cast you into hell! I die to live
who will bring *you* back to life?

Against this another whirls in a frenzied controlled dance
he dreams on orgies dark forces revolve
demons
incinerations of the spirit
the Bomb
in its mushroom flower actions round a dumb Black Angel cloud

3

I have never made a poem never emerged it's all a farce
    if I could unravel as this Raga into song
opulent view of Kashmir
thousands of images bearing light
light thru clouds the beauty of things
lit up slow unraveling of the morning

On a himalaya
this one in sight of heaven
outpouring
prayer of lungs sex eyes
eyes poured in abysms of light

the flight of horned heads
gods, cats, bulls, dogs, sphinxes
each head inside out a torso of fish

        Ranka uraniku
        bahaba hi olama
        sancu pantis droga
        harumi pahunaka

I never see enough
with those who fly tortoise shell in the infinite hangup
words slow unraveling song

the gods are vomiting
I am entering earth I am walled in light I am where the song is
    shot into my eyes *O hypodermic light!*

FROM THE FRONT

Tenochtitlan!
grey seven thousand feet high
mist of dust—tin door open
to slow motion immobilized traffic
—girl at window—terrace—
terrace a heartmobile—
wind! dust of wind—wind!

sail of dead ghost opium people
fantast—the fields of Egluria

these watches promote me
Venetian blinds, Chicagos of Zeno

The mountain erupts
landmasses grab the Pacific
earthquakes
the sky is peeling its skin off!

Is this American mood? 1960 weather beasts,
    who tampers the moon tides?

Reprieve. Sail of dust wind
venetian mountain sequence
zeroguns silence the street
mute traffics—desperate surrealism
backfire from motorcycles
waves over empty roof tops

Geneva of movies, who ate the dogbrick sandwich ?
I've cut a loaf of it
and splattered eiou—chaos
slamming Venetian blinds
click, the cat asleep
        aloha, tidal waves

Where am I ? you answer
the question where am I ?
who's here? who wants Veracruz?
what is New York? who is San Francisco?
Friend
where are you?
what to do   go where   how?

Motorcycles of atonal venetian blind dust of wind roof top!

THE THIRD EYE

        Contra Satanas—
    thy light is higher than light, angels
brighter than angels
                Moons whisper their lights
  it's the end of the world
Fasting and reborn, the Crystal forms out of moonlight & sunlight
Day and night, Green Crystal Red White Black Blue CRYSTAL!
        Yellow Crystal!
         Brown Crystal!

    I am Hymnon riding hamwings of Aquarius,
  beards of Samothrace, jonquils
        from deserts of the sea

    In my nights of white photography mountains fell
  my heads rolled dice in heaven, my eyes poured out poison
In my day of love I saw   one rock
        one strata   one pinnacle   one tree
            one vine   one sprig of green
                one flower   one woman I loved
  I am Pythagoras agitator smiling from infinite blue coins
        I am paid by light

        light
        is
        house
        of
        MINT!

Garden   Light
 of   of the   my finger is God!
his monies   garden

 Waves
    Waves   Waves
     Waves   Waves

—it's indescript! I've gone into inaudia!
   Maldororian waves! Angel I've seen
     angel I haven't seen
   light of darkness
      visitation of noname about to smash
    into *smiles*
 Here is face of old water man buried
     in quickgreen lime fountains of
Zut Gut
   accent over "u"
   the waves
      photojournal   seascape
              fin.

Secret Freedom

BLUE GRACE

              crashes thru air
where Lady LSD hangs up all the floors of life for the last time
Blue Grace leans on white slime
Blue Grace weaves in & out of Lüneburg and "My Burial Vault"
    undulates
from first hour peyote turnon
Diderot hand in hand with the Marquis de Sade
wraps himself up in a mexican serapé
at Constitution Hall, Philadelphia, 1930

Blue Grace turns into the Count of Saint-Germain
      who lives forever
           cutting up George Washington
dream of pyramid liquefactions from thighs of Versailles

Blue Grace intimidates Nevil Chamberlain
feels up Fillippo Marinetti
and other hysterics of the phallic rose

Blue Grace dressed up as automobile sperm
    My Claw of the future
      and the almond rose Rich the Vampire wears
                    over the US Army
—FLAGS!
        AMERICAN FLAGS!
  flying like bats
             out of "My Burial Vault"!
flood museums
          where Robespierre's murder is plotted
              —floated from Texcoco,

the Prince of Bogota caught redhanded
sniffing forty cans of Berlin ether!

                  Hydrek ice blue teeth
           impersonates, psycho-kinetically,
the resurrection of Blue Grace as prophetess of the anti-planet
   system

Blue Grace under dark glasses
getting out of one hundred white cars at once!
Cars of ectoplasmic tin-types
go to the juncture where Blue Grace Glass is raped
      at the Court of Miracles, Mexico City, 1959

Blue Grace undressed
reveals tattoo marks of Hamburg, sea & storm of
                    Neptune-Pluto conjunction
Rumors of war
strafe the automation monster
walking to universal assassination
K & K and the russian poets
suck Blue Grace's opulent morsels, back & front
The nicotine heaven of Bosch's painting
emanates the thousand beauties of
    Christopher Maclaine's tool box
of mechanical brass jewels
                  Man,
                  the marvel
                  of masturbation arts,
          intersects Blue Grace
    at World's Finale Orgasm Electro-Physic Apocalypse!

I sing the beauty of bodily touch
with my muse, Blue Grace

                                              (Spring 1963)

The sun is bleeding over the sky!

The sun is bleeding over the sky!
Beauty be my prophecy and
youth my analog of wisdom,
to strike notes of wild wondrous song
where the rays of childwood eyes
extend far beyond the enemies of all natural ecstasy!

Youth's dream that zaps the zepher
of galactic sex! Youth's flood
of rapture's delight
that intercepts the candle of the sky
and rolls up its fire into balls of tropic night
lightning down the grey monsters of rational crime

Oh! Go out to the end of the world, Hands
of my surrealist youth! When all the trees
bent to thy rites
of savage runes and flights the sunbird made
on midnight's exploded jewel!

Diamond eye of rocket heads of youth!
Flame brain that banished the horizon
with a fourteen year old Scowl
of the Sibyl's spear
crashing down to living death
those who'd stop my march
to the rawmeat city of Flame-Sea-Sun-Ecstasy!

Ah, that I never forget thee, wonderwood
of phosgene youth! When forests of ink
flamed to golden goblets that sang my heart's
pure leap into the blood war rings of Thor!

Over the hill of windy rages
from the whorl of eucalyptic green
the voice of Ariel Morgenroth
did come down and bade me sing
the kingdom of Elsewhere off the shores of Never More;
it was and IS the moment you can not compass
—from materia prima to the specular stone—
where I kindle this paper
over pyres of prophecy:

Youth's dream
    to burn down the dreads of dope
        and dour old men's sickly sex
           and sicker greeds!

THE ANCIENTS HAVE RETURNED AMONG US

in a way humming thru crystals of light—most unexpected—
    the ancients sizzle and dazzle
not as we imagined nor can put our machines to nor
    make comprehensible by words or songs or metaphors
    The ancients have truly returned to us
    and have unfurled flags of sudden Cloud Rings
    from rivers crossing the most ordinary streets
on the way back from mediterranean flowers whose lips
sip the leaf-elevators of the natural man buried in the
dreams whose chrysalis snaps from the Dragon
    of fortuitous events whispered at the Age of Cham
& sent hurtling from the steeples of Og
    I can hear the ancients from the mouth of
 fog &   dazzling wind sonatas beloved of hunchback adepts
& dismembered mummies whose Living Light
    crackles from the diapason of This Constant Present Moment
    they use as a bridge to remind me to be silent
    & seal my words by carbon honeys & not to spare
    the endless rolls of cellophane reaching Saturn
    by the cross-fibred necropolis of the Hanged Man:
    they caution me to Flamboyant Order
that repeats the dooms ordained by the transfiguration
    of the banners of wayward heralds whose brains
    fall blandly & sedately & fall again
through the overdrenched factories of neon blindness
& who cares? since it is all known to have been
fixed in the calendars of the Twins & read
    throughout prehistory from the Secret Stones
cast on the Shadow: The ancients have returned

      & unfurl repeatedly into your Ear the scroll
    of living legends, the talk of multiplying flowers
foamed over books without words in libraries
        built by fire to the laboratory that dissolves
      constantly into an ocean of anti-matter
Truly the wisdom of the ancients is written everywhere you can
      not see it and
secreted nowhere other than through the tachygraph
      under the cascade of capillary mountains
forever registered before this instant gave birth to
its opposite which is snaking beyond the distance
        between you and I moonman & opal of the sun
This arrangement by special decree of what
    turns night into day or brings the longest night
before the Lion that rips open the throat of the New Year
    when the ancients were the youngest gods burst
    from the bubbles of sperm spit   Listen!
their music played from buzz & bleats
    you can not hear except through periscopes
      set down among vascular whales
mating from the crisis of rock & shale under
    the disappearing atlantis of corn cultures &
reappearing before the wheat altars on
      the plains of the western wind & western winter from
      which the words & letters were handed down
    the elevators of Tomorrow over the Deluge
the great night giant sends us today by blood-lined
cups swollen with ichor & flames throbbed from
      lyres lost to
      Sothis & returning from under that Sea
whose waves break from the Iris of the Ibis:
      These cups that flow like banners of molten lead

> Cups put together by Tartesian Giants
> hallucinated by the saints of Ys
> unveiled in allegories of the Tower floating the
> hearts of children
> cups whose brims overcrowd now the rustling autumn
> Door to the invisible temple built unseen
> in the cities of the Satanic machine
> Cups the legends reveal & the ancients
> are beginning to pass around as if they were ordinary
> milk bottles for the children newly born from
> top branches of the Tree with its roots
> going back
> to the starfields of Every Night.

SHE SPEAKS THE MORNING'S FILIGREE

Beneath him, earth's breath
risen from inward wars of blood:
the youth's vision
is a vibrant string plucked by the gods
over the field of stars

Through the night on fire with my blood
whose incense sputters your sleep and washes you
on the threshold caught from the Tinging Stone
I'm tired of cooking the ultimate specter of future poems
weak from demands of the mooneating children of the 25th
    Century
it's really so late to proclaim my youth of a hundred years!

But you, Io,
walking on sandals of almond & wrapped by hair of eglantine,
open the scashell that sings us back through storms of smoke
to the burnt altars of childhood that float
in milk I drew from dragons slain with the help of the sylph:
Clocks rant their dirges of woe to no avail!

Your sleep is my awakening
All the shadows lie canceled by celestial foam
Moon-poisons are cooked to the perfection of Tea
The sun stirs the cauldron Sothis fixes from your tears
that dance as diamonds on opalescent hands breaking the Seven
    Seals!
Over & over the dusk of the Chant from the plain of Segovia
rings up the veil through which the deities move prisms of desire:
the cup that swallows the sword, the wands that shake the stars!

Aurora the cat of the morning
has sent a message of aerial fire
to the twelve-faced Aerolith whose name is not permitted for reading
whose number is water & abyss of the bone
whose age is always about to become and
has always been no less than time

We can play host to the marvelous
and have it burn us to the salt of memory
where an invisible stone contracts all thought
to draw out the words
that shall crackle your sleep
to wake us up beyond the Pleiades

No longer tired now I've supt from the tombs of kings
and raced past the Giant Chairs of Tartesos
to mark the spectrum's path to where you and I
shall be buried in the seed of the Sun
I'm at the gate of the house built by no one
but the One who pulled it down
before it was founded from the sperm of the walking sleeper!
From this place my poems can begin
to take on the shape of candles
    and incense sticks

> *as you ride midnight mares*
> *to undo the astral curse*
>   *turn pages of burning books*
>   *or float*
>   *freely*
> *on the mornings filigree!*

GORK!

Or, My Personal Minute Reading On the Calendar of Emblems Proclaimed From the *Principality of Weir* Which is *Constantly SomeWhereElse,* Therefor Unreachable by Machines & Beyond Any Psycho-Physical Analysis, and Conjuncts Only *Relatively* With the Phantomatic Distortions & Material Encumbrances Socially Projected by Over Proliferating Mobocracies, Murderous & Degenerate Sciences, Retrograde Religions & Politics At This Time Increasingly Oppressive & Horent Perpetuating Their Arbitrary Prerogatives Out of Certain *Atavisms of Thought & Operation*—Steeped in Integral Errors—*Known* to Corrupt and Destroy Our Humanity.

★

It's one of those days when the moon jumps
out of its skin and the walls of the sky
crash down with a thud
of Saturn's rings: from the wind
that drops its eggs to the gull
who hatches them from its gullet

It's one of those days govern
ments war on the earth's dinner tables
& heads of state are venus fly traps
eating the scum of their slaves
from cisterns of all the phony capitols
of King Mob

It's one of those days I'd as soon the electrons
fell out of their atoms
or never move across my room except
to play endlessly *The Art*

of the Fugue since it's on a day like this
the planetary aspects are so bad if
anyone at all is not a Taoist—Be Still
& Act Not—an age of karma is set going so that
all future cranes & paradise birds
over bleed on the crests of all the seas
of our world, to the degree that on
Another One of These Days the air itself
shall strike down the citizens like a plague!

For it was on one of these days
the Perfect One degenerated into a
crocodile and the Sylphs of old
mated with the baboons who oozed up from
the Crash of the Eighth Moon!
                    (Sagittarius Decan I 10th Day 1965)

VOICE OF EARTH MEDIUMS

We are truly fed up
with mental machines of peace & war
nuclear monoxide brains, cancerous computers
motors sucking our hearts of blood
that once sang the choruses of natural birds!
We've had enough dynamos & derricks
thud-thud-thudding valves & pulleys
of the Devil Mankin's invention
                And soon
if they aren't *silenced*
and we survive the sacrificial altars
of the automobile god and the vulvas of steel
spitting molecular madness
through layers of satanic dust

if the complete crowd-manacled Machine
isn't *dissolved, back into the Earth*
from where its elements were stolen
                we shall call on
the Great Ocean Wave
Neter of waters
and the King of Atlantis & his snake-spirits
otherwise known as
                Orcus
                Dagon & Drack!
to send up calamitous tidal waves
—a thousand feet high, if need be—
to bury all the monster metal cities
and their billion, bullioned wheels of chemical death!

Oh, William Blake!
thou can overseer, if it please thee,
this lesson of Aquarius Clean Sweep
that Earth's beautiful spirit of purifying Ocean
shall stop these weights on and plunder of
her metal blood and very thin skin
to teach us Terra's song of taoist harmonies!

WHAT IS NOT STRANGE?

Sea towers of Sicily
  change place with the tongues
    of elephants borne on the back
      of the Ibis
        What is *not* strange
          among eddies of the
            hermaphrodite
              caught on the spiked hair
              of foam—your lips, Diotima
              result from the broken statues
            of Hermes & open
          with the click
        of all the fans of Murasaki
      What is not strange is
    that
the shorelines of zipzap cities
explode giant coke bottles
  lighting the savage factories
    supercharging
      morning blur to
        Venus—Ping!
          Visionary hotrodders
              tear off their clothes before you, Geronimo:
            Epiphany
              in a starspangled leather jacket
                flapping on the hammocks
                  of the bivouac girls
                    back from their raids on the moon.

What is *not* strange
opening up sassafras seeds,
golden whistles and millenniums
of Pest at a single glance from Superman
—he who is not coming back ever—
as the Holy Biscuits
spill endlessly dollar bills the future
shall print their poems on!
What is not strange?
now that I've swallowed the Pacific Ocean
and sabotaged the Roman Empire
and you have returned
from all your past lives
to sip the snakes of my fingertips:

Go Away & Be Born No More!

DO A KUNDALINI SOMERSAULT!

GOTHIC GAMES

1

When they do come bearing midnight suppers
wrought from Merlin's gobble machine
let it be hands *not bleeding at the wrists*
but slightly invisible
say clothed in a miniature seafoam cloudette

hands that slip elegantly
    out of the air
and let the dishes be chafing, but
bearing hamburgers with relish
and frankfurters from WunderbarLand!

2

Take a trip into the grail legend
eschew those dull "responsible" profiteers
who'd nourish you on video plastics
Here
at the castle
it's sunbeams for breakfast
and opal meat for lunch
dinner is unspeakable
and *secret*
but this much I can tell you:
the nutrition so ethereal
spiration alone accomplishes digestion
and the bloodstream transmuted
into a cascade of celestial fluids

Naturally
all is served from invisible hands
with a complete spectrum of sound
interlaced with each bite

From the walls, lips—
shaped like moon changes—
sing harmonies arranged from the
chaos of that *other* world
beyond the submerged forest where,
it is said, those who were once men
now become slaves of their inventions
conspire sinister dragons rocketing
out of elsewhere to nowhere.

TOWERS OF THE ROSE DAWN

Having lived
for a long time on each side of
the bridge within sight of three towers
it was only after the bridge fell
thunderously into the water
that a great wave rose

to carry me safely
before the four doors of the castle
and spill into my hands, a giant key
inscribed with the weir-image of the head & eyes
of a green and beautiful beast.

CAPRICORN IS A WOUNDED KNEE

No wonder the night is smeared with ectoplasm
eagle's blood flows over the planets
and we cast a spell for seven hawks to fly out of the moon
that silence may prevail
to so startle the noisy villagers
for us to hear the songs that break
from the lips of the air

ASTRO-MANCY

The stars have gone crazy
and the moon is very angry
The old civilization
that rolled the dice of Hitler
is surely bumbling
into a heap of catatonic hysteria
Another civilization
secret for six thousand years
is creeping on the crest of
future, I can almost see the
tip of its triangular star
I'm writing this from lost Atlantis
I wonder when I'll get back
to the alchemical castle
where I can rebegin my work
left off in the Middle Ages
when the Black Beast roared down
on my weedy parchments and spilled me
into an astral waiting room
whose angels, naturally in flaming white robes,
evicted me for this present irony:
idleness, mancy & The Dream
instead of getting down to
the super-real work of
transmuting the Earth *with love of it*
by the Fire prepared from the time of Onn!
No matter, I'm recovering
from a decade of poisons
I renounce all narcotic
& pharmacopoeic disciplines

as too heavy 9-to-5-type sorrows
Instead I see America
as one vast palinode
that reverses itself completely until
Gitchi Manito actually returns
as prophet of a new Iroquois Brotherhood—
this needs further development—
I forsee a couple of
essential changes:
a Break Out Generation
of poet-kings setting up
The Realm Apart
of sweet natural play
and light metal work
matter lovingly heightened
by meditation, and spirit
transmuted into matter,
the whole commune conducted by
direct rapid transcription
from a no-past reference
anti-rational, fantastically poetic
violently passive and
romantically unprejudiced
Each one his own poet
and poetry the central fact
food & excrement of culture
I see you smiling tolerantly
O liberal lip (another utopian
bites the dust) but no! you just
can't see what I'm reading while
in the act of transcribing it
know at least three other

supernatural souls who envision
much the same under different names,
but the nomenclature's not more than
the lucid panorama I telescope
as, on this summer night's
torpor, it passes from under my eyelid and

grabs you, earth returned,
into the middle of Aquarius, one millennium forward.

AFTER THE VIRUS

Am I happy? Were I happy!
Zoos of happiness converge
on horrors which is a wide paw
of who calls first from
the lip's underscore
Happiness not a constant state
The field of man's gore
makes bones shine further
to the suicide machine
We make the sacrifice tree grow
for its necessary leavens
burnished with an ecstatic smile
of pain—the oscillations escalate—
not a moment of happiness but
contradicted by the black undertow
What, then, is coming to be
from undergrounds too fast
in their bright plumages
flailing our brains
with the gash of birth?
Something storing mercurial islets
and fungi of being . . .
and sold for altars
pitched to the stars!

COAT OF ARMS

Pure as gale and mist washing my skull
pure as silk dances on the ocean's knee
    thong thighs of the walking coast
pure as Mendocino witch havens
    through the transparent plumes of extinct birds
looking down from the sky-people boat
exploding over candy castles
    the salt wisdom pervades
safe as the mummy's purity *is* from the congresses of fear

The night goes up
into the ventricles of King Novalis
and horned men descend the saline stairway
whose bones are lit up from astral lamps
of the great genii, Ignis phana, pure claw
that brushes death's meat
awakened without a body on the edge of the clubfooted wave

Going around blind corners, the sylph
breaks her teeth on the borders of three continents
I pass without passports—
rapid vision overtakes the storm
of this glittering void I love
and reveals everything in a speeding cloud!

This is the moral for inventing ecstasies
Freed from the clutch of memory
I eat the eagle's windy branches
    my eye the lion's cave
silver fluids fix my voice
that sings *The World and I Are One!*
What's newly hatched is born from dying seed!

To let loose a room's inner skeleton
I come from far places
dressed in the explosions of green lamps
It's the moment before arson
Taught not to look back
my fires drink a porous stone
    The geyser speaks
    at the house of the onyx mirror
    My name is augur
    these lips besmirch the dawn
    My sword's a vaporous cloud
The tooth marks of ecstasy
wear the look of totems
and the dragon's vermouth tongue
Every arm is bathed in silver blood
    I read the spells of Egypt patiently

Even if I could not reach you, *supreme opal*,
the carnivorous sea is avenged
even if you erased the cornerstone of the temple
against the door melting with pride
I would marry all the stars sitting on the face of the sea
like a traditional wolf of the absolute
sucking down the dish served up by the flood!

O ponder the gaze of the forest!
Raise mist from the shore!
There's this gull punished by clouds
on the inevitable hour of genetic infantries
and a war on oracles
After history has washed her head
the grail heroes move over gigantic chess sets

Am I passive enough yet
to breathe the fire of the opal?
And walk over my graves
that withstood the cleavages of insect wars?
To wake up from death, *satisfied*

   the forest before me
replaced
        by a cartilage of stars?

DIFFICULT FIRST STEPS

1

It comes over me like a gigantic faun web
of intricate dance and rouses black fire
Not yet prepared, but for
the clutter of baneful voices
I run the risk of being cut down
by the charging beasts of good sense
I have been nervous before
Human beans made me sick
and vampires insinuated themselves
too long into the crevices of my inner lodes
I shall take care not to listen to them again!

2

There is only this black ice forest
to whet my appetite as it leans
its invisible breasts for the
gelatinous lurch of my mind
I am not the first nor the last
to start off for this splendorous x-ray road
for which the universe was made
The swords of entire enchantment
cut the weeds overgrowing its hair
At each step I'm fortified
—when miraculous fingers
rend the mist we inherit from spirit-mongers
to keep us from the hungry foods—
by those whom we have yet to meet
and were not, as we, born from mineral minions.

3

There are mines of mysterious moments
that open their tentacular veins
dropping flowers with which the worker
threads his probes to uncover calyx
come from outer space—
x-ray visioned, their stamens
entwine us with other worlds
though we can not see them
as they shed the black light of dreams
Or now they come looking
into angel-swung litanies the sea irradiates
at the hilt of any night
in a jungle of black waves
that pour you, spines and vocal suns,
a caustic air
that spins me to the rock of enigmatic love,
affinities of the mineral diving board
that is my body contracting to the rhythm
of its murex hand churning the waters below
and only the starlight consoles.

Afterword

The Hand Set Free to Dream: The Correspondence of Philip Lamantia and Lawrence Ferlinghetti

The surviving correspondence between Lawrence Ferlinghetti and Philip Lamantia concerning the latter's first volume in the Pocket Poets Series, *Selected Poems: 1943–1966* (City Lights, 1967), is surprisingly robust. From the mid-1950s to the late 1960s, Lamantia led a peripatetic existence in Mexico, Europe, and Morocco, and a trunk containing much of his own record of his correspondence was lost during his deportation from Mexico in 1962. By 1966, however, when he began assembling *Selected Poems*, he was living in more stable circumstances, in the town of Nerja, Malaga, on the Mediterranean coast of Spain. Some of this stability derived from his relationship with Nancy Joyce Peters, whom he had met the year before in Athens and would eventually marry after their return to the United States. With Peters's encouragement, Lamantia fully reembraced the surrealism of his youth, and, periods of silence notwithstanding, he would maintain this allegiance for the rest of his life.

One question I've long had, given that Ferlinghetti began City Lights Publishing in 1955, is why he didn't publish Lamantia in the Pocket Poets Series until 1967. Ferlinghetti had met both Lamantia and Robert Duncan as early as 1954[1] at one of Kenneth Rexroth's Friday soirees and published Duncan's *Selected Poems* as Pocket Poets Number 10 in 1959. What I failed to consider is that the impediment lay much more on Lamantia's end. The gap between his first book, *Erotic Poems* (Bern Porter Editions, 1946), and his second book, *Ekstasis* (Auerhahn Press, 1959), wasn't for want of opportunity or material, but rather was due to the poet's highly mercurial nature. Books were even announced—such as *Expel the Green Pain* (1953) from Jack Stauffacher's Greenwood Press or

---

1. See Ferlinghetti's "Foreword" to *The Collected Poems of Philip Lamantia* (California, 2013), p. xix.

Tau (1955)[2] from Bern Porter—but Lamantia would cancel them before they saw the light of day, due to his evolving beliefs about spirituality and about poetry itself.

But while his correspondence from this period is mostly lost, the City Lights archive—housed, along with Lamantia's, at the Bancroft Library at the University of California, Berkeley—contains two letters and a postcard from Philip indicating that he and Ferlinghetti also discussed doing a project as early as 1959. In the first letter, dated April 15, 1959 and sent from Mexico City, Lamantia writes:

> Soon, within a month I suspect (if Ekstasis appears by then!) I can have ready for you, not Destroyed Works (which is not completed as a BOOK) but, rather, APOCALYPSES which contains one poem of 2 pages, 'Opus Magnum' that may be the greatest poem I've ever been able to write, as well as 'Press-Release' 3 Manifestos, and a short shot re junk scene n/y/c 1949... / this totals about 8 ms pages / could be done, i suggest, as a broadside for City Lights / Pocket Books[.]

He also proposes "certain letters of Artaud together to be called ARTAUD NARCOTICS, or A DEMAND FOR EXTINCTION OF LAWS PROHIBITING NARCOTIC MEDICINES.....this should be ready within two months, that is, in translation process now!" Those familiar with Lamantia's bibliography will undoubtedly be intrigued by this snapshot of his intentions. *Ekstasis* did appear later that year from Dave Haselwood's Auerhahn Press; on the book's front cover flap, *Apocalypses* is announced as "In retort," though it never appeared as such. "Opus Magnum,"

---

2. While three of its poems—"Intersection," "Terror Conduction," and "Man Is in Pain"—were included in *Ekstasis*, *Tau* was eventually published in full by City Lights as part of Pocket Poets No. 59, *Tau* by Philip Lamantia and *Journey to the End* by John Hoffman (2008). Another poem from *Tau*, "The Owl," made its first book appearance in *Touch of the Marvelous* (Oyez, 1966) before appearing the next year in *Selected Poems*.

however, would later appear in the "Mantic Notebook" section of *Destroyed Works* (Auerhahn, 1962), grouped with other poems under the subhead "The Apocalyptic," suggesting that the *Apocalypses* project was incorporated into this book. As for "A DEMAND," one recognizes an early concept for *Narcotica* (Auerhahn, 1959), which ultimately contained translations of only a pair of Artaud texts ("A Letter to the Legislator of the Law on Narcotics" and "General Security—The Liquidation of Opium") and Leopardi's "The Infinite," but otherwise consisted of Lamantia's own drug manifestoes and poems. Indeed, the *Narcotica* translation of "General Security" would later appear in City Lights' *Artaud Anthology* (1962), suggesting Lamantia as a source for Ferlinghetti's interest in the French writer.

Ferlinghetti's reply to this letter is lost, but that there was a reply is indicated by a short follow-up postcard from Lamantia also postmarked 1959. But the next missive from Philip in the City Lights archive comes from Mexico City in March 1961. By then, he had already given Haselwood and Auerhahn *Destroyed Works*, which, much to the poet's chagrin, wouldn't appear until 1962. In the meantime, he proposes a new project: "it's a shorter thing, up to 35 pages of pocketbk size, with this title I think you'll dig: REVOLUTIONS OF THE ANARCHIST KING—also containing a few pages of, with prose explanation, of a new sonic language, 'babbel'—" Four paragraphs later he adds that he "may do a long 5 page poem of prophetic mantic politico—visionary—title: Kosmos—that'll be in Revolutions too..."

Revolutions of the Anarchist King falls under the category of books Lamantia planned but didn't announce; these books manifest on certain of his typescripts as handwritten designations of the project for which the poem was intended, rather than as fully arranged manuscripts. Both "Kosmos," a poem seemingly recounting an experience of ego death through the use of a hallucinogen, and "Babbel," a group of sound poems accompanied by his explanation of their origins, are among the previously unpublished work included in Lamantia's *Collected Poems*

(California, 2013).[3] In light of this letter, the internal connection between "Kosmos" and "Babbel" becomes obvious; in one line of "Kosmos," he launches into some "Babbel"-like syllables ("come to guard sweet melting mountain come to third-eyed castle come maruna comana alora tumari ceona"), though he had had such wordless passages in his work as early as *Narcotica*. But a later line of "Kosmos," I now realize, contains a direct reference: "my words destroyed in babbel burning air! one tongue of tongues!" If Ferlinghetti weighed in on this proposed MS, that letter disappeared with Lamantia's trunk in 1962; after his return to surrealism, in any case, Lamantia lost interest in most of his then-published work, never revisiting "Kosmos" despite its undeniable ambition and power and its self-evidently surrealist imagery.

These preliminaries aside, the project that became *Selected Poems* begins in earnest with a letter dated August 26, 1966 that Ferlinghetti sent to Lamantia in Nerja.

> Allen [Ginsberg] showed me yr letter & I am eager to do a book of yours[.] (It's about time! What?) What about SELECTED POEMS OF PHILIP LAMANTIA or wd you prefer something wilder & more beautiful? I wd quote your letter to Allen in a little note at the beginning: "I believe, more than ever, that there is *something else*, and that It is within us, your Flower, my Fire, Blake's Genius, the *ka* of Egypt, the One Thing of Trismegistus...and it can be *transmitted* & survive in the Great Return to the Source......................God, of course, does not exist—the Unique *is*, though, we continue...." (I have made a copy of this page of yr letter/hope you don't mind.) Call the book THE POETIC TRANCE?—from yr phrase in letter "The Poetic Trance for me is the place of locating" ???? Of course, I wouldn't use any of this unless you dug....It's

---

[3]. I should note that my co-editors and I placed the "Babbel" poems in the wrong section of the *Collected Poems* ("Poems 1963–1964" instead of "Poems 1955–1962"); sometimes we had to guess!

> yr book, you make it, I'll print it, I mean publish it.....So
> yr bk cud be "new work" or collected "old" work....Let
> me hear....

The quotation from Lamantia's letter to Ginsberg is tantalizing, given that the letter itself seems to be lost. Among the Ginsberg papers housed in the Special Collections at the Stanford Library, there's a two-year gap in correspondence from Lamantia, from October 30, 1964 to October 25, 1966, a good two months after Ferlinghetti quotes the letter in question, and the quotation doesn't appear in the earlier correspondence.[4] Judging by the timing, however, and the quotation itself—concerning the generative impulse behind his poems, which he conceived of as automatic *transmission* rather than deliberate composition—I presume this lost letter detailed Lamantia's return to surrealism some 20 years after he had renounced it.

By 1965, Lamantia had begun composing new surrealist poems. The next year, Robert Hawley's Oyez Press published *Touch of the Marvelous*, a gathering of Lamantia's earliest surrealist work, written between 1943 and 1945 when he was still a teenager. Included among these poems are the ones he published in Charles Henri Ford and Parker Tyler's magazine *View* and André Breton's surrealist journal in exile, *VVV*. Perhaps due to this new edition of his first poems, Lamantia at first demurred on the idea of a selected poems, writing back on September 8, 1966:

> What I have in mind [for City Lights] is a book of
> work done in the past year or so (after relative silence
> of 3 years)—to date, this would come to only about 30
> pages, buk-wise, but the vein that's been opened for
> me—recently—promises to open WIDER and so I'd

---

4. On this point, I need to extend my deepest thanks to Tim Noakes of the Stanford University Special Collections, who went out of his way over the Christmas/New Year holidays of 2023 to communicate with me regarding Lamantia's correspondence in the Ginsberg archives.

> like to have another month or two to supplement what I already have: including last months most exciting aperture where I flowed for about 10 pages and gave me a tentative title for the whole book: THE HAND SET FREE TO DREAM. Though I have alternate ideas for titles, including MAGICAL HAPPENINGS—which up until this new long poem, I had thought described the other twenty pages made up of about 8 shorter ones....

Lamantia doesn't fully abandon the idea of *some* selection from his earlier work, however, "say about 15–20 pages of the purest surreal ones," in order to "make up an integral volume for City Lights[.]" Still, it's by no means clear to me what poems Lamantia is referring to here by "this new long poem" and the "8 shorter ones." Intriguingly, there is a folder among his papers labeled "Selected Poems 1943–1966, Typescript & Notes" that doesn't contain any of the final book. Rather, it is mostly handwritten pages, sometimes drafting lines for poems and sometimes recording his attempts to work out, say, a part title for a section of the book. The folder also contains typescripts of multiple abandoned attempts to draft a statement to preface *Selected Poems* and reaffirm his allegiance to surrealism.

Of the typescripts that do appear in this folder, only one seems to be complete. "World Without End," a long prose poem that ends Lamantia's subsequent full-length collection of new work, *The Blood of the Air* (Four Seasons, 1970), appears here as a six-page lineated typescript, giving some indication of the extent to which he might rework a poem, even as he insisted on the automatic and unconscious origin of its initial inspiration. "If a poem is not written in a state of passion—what we used to call the zone—" he later remarked, "then forget it."[5] Aside from "World Without End," the typescripts in this folder are fragmentary. There are what I'm guessing are three related pages, one of which

---

5. "Surrealism & Mysticism" in Philip Lamantia, *Preserving Fire: Selected Prose* (Wave Books, 2018), 146.

bears the title "Exorcism of the Inner Itch." Other fragments are much shorter, including eight typed lines labeled "V (nov. 2 version)":

> O poor astral anatomy!
> so long bludgeoned by occult blows
> But nothing can stop the eternal loin
> from speaking its ocean to be
> I can barely see you
> and mixed up to be chopped
> like so many valentine hearts
> by the fierce blades I roll out of the black star!

and another five typed lines dated "nov. 30 66":

> emblazoned with the thunder's kiss
> we are wild to surpass
> bloody neons & cigarette cities
> emblazoned with twilight of moons
> we've overgrown

Linking these two fragments is a third, heavily hand-edited page dated "Nov. 2" also containing the phrase "bloody neons." This is curious, given the existence of a poem, "Mumbles," whose first section is titled "Bloody Neons," which Lamantia printed in a 1965 magazine he and the Greek surrealist Nanos Valaoritis published called *Residu*. This raises a probably unanswerable question: was Lamantia still working on "Mumbles" with an eye towards building the volume of recent work he describes to Ferlinghetti?[6]

As it happened, Ferlinghetti sent a postcard to Lamantia on the morning of September 13, reiterating his desire to publish

---

6. Complicating matters even further is a letter from Lamantia to Ferlinghetti dated July 10, 1967—after the appearance of *Selected Poems*—in which Philip mentions "two longish poems" he's still working on, "Epiphany" and "Host of Prophecies," though it's unclear whether these are the same long poems he referred to before they settle on the idea of a selected poems. I don't think either of these poems survive. "Mumbles" appears in the *Collected Poems* (pp. 214–220).

a "selected poems," only to receive Philip's above-quoted letter of the 8th that afternoon. Ferlinghetti thus dispatched another letter, also dated the 13th, in which he accedes to *The Hand Set Free to Dream* proposal. Lamantia's reply, however, is dated October 25, a delay he attributes to an extended bout of illness (caused, he writes, by "BUGS," seemingly an intestinal parasite). In this letter, he proposes a new title, *The Absolute Trip*, evoking not only his own wandering but also the burgeoning psychedelic culture of which he himself had been an intrepid pioneer. In his November 1 response, Ferlinghetti remains open to the volume Lamantia suggests, but makes one last attempt to rescue the "selected" proposal:

> This makes me wonder if you should not reconsider calling our volume SELECTED POEMS and going through *all* your work to-date, including unpublished poetry, to make a comprehensive selection of say 80 or even 100 pages, solid. It's really not too early to do that. (We did it with Duncan's SELECTED POEMS, and he was quite happy with it for a number of years, until he'd produced so much new work that that volume had no more validity as a "selected" receuil....)[.] Or even make your book COLLECTED POEMS. Why not? You wouldn't have to include everything published anyway. Yet you could make the book as big as you wanted: 150 pages, for instance. [. . .] Think it over. I think either SELECTED or COLLECTED wd make a more important book, in fact a very significant book, rather than another collection or choix based upon a title-theme.....

As an editor, I can't fail to be moved by Lawrence's generosity and tact. If he believed in a poet, he was all in, and here he throws himself and his press at Philip's disposal, even if it means following Lamantia down a rabbit hole akin to the unrealized proposals of '59 and '61. But Ferlinghetti was correct to point out the greater impact a selected would have, and his good sense prevails here;

Lamantia immediately writes back on November 7, calling the selected "a very good idea." "I am most enthusiastic about your projection of it being a 'significant' volume—at last!" he admits, sensible of his dissatisfaction with his previous volumes.[7] By the same token, he shows little enthusiasm for a "collected":

> But I guess you meant in terms of a Collected edition
> that include *everything* from a book; but actually I really
> would prefer to make a selection of what I do consider—
> now with the distance of decades, or half-decades
> between their original publication & now—to be the
> *highest* or best level of the whole output, rather than
> print a lot of stuff that I later regret having to look at
> again in a book!

This seals the deal. Ferlinghetti replies on November 16: "Groove-city. That's fine, I'm glad you agree to SELECTED POEMS & here is real contract for same," sketching out the basic terms and asking for a manuscript by the end of December. He also inquires whether Philip was interested in a photo cover, like "the type used on the Oyez cover," or would prefer to "stick to the typographical type cover used so far in the Pocket Poets." In his November 22 reply, Lamantia opts for "your 'distinctive' & typographical cover":

> Besides think your classic one advantageous as for
> recognition-sake. Black & white would be o.k., though
> since Allen's books with you are in that combination you
> might not prefer that, so then some kind of Blood RED
> border, with black lettering for title & poet's name on
> white background would be most suitable, I feel, similar
> to [Gregory Corso's] who told me last year in Paris: "You
> are a blood poet"—and that may be right!

---

7. In a sense, Lamantia's first three full-length volumes—*Erotic Poems*, *Ekstasis*, and *Destroyed Works*—were all made from the wreckage of previous unrealized conceptions for books.

This is exactly what the design of the final book—which, like *Howl* and the other early Pocket Poets, was printed letterpress by Villiers in London—would turn out to be. Ferlinghetti wouldn't abandon the idea of photo covers, however, simultaneously issuing Bob Kaufman's *Golden Sardine* with a photo of the poet on the cover.[8]

This letter from Lamantia also lands on the book's full title, *Selected Poems 1943–1966*, adding the years so "the book will stand as a definitive selection for the *actual* period it covers, and can't be immediately superseded [sic], being truly & openly-stated selection in a cumulative sense, and will stand beyond even a future book or books City Lights may eventually publish of mine!" Yet in a move characteristic of Philip's indecisiveness concerning the presentation of his poetry in book form, by the end of the letter, he's convinced himself the book should be called *Wild Minutes: Selected Poems 1943–1966*. The record is silent as to whether Ferlinghetti dissuaded him from this title or whether Lamantia simply abandoned the idea; the month-long gap between this letter and the next suggests that some correspondence was lost. Suffice to say, *Wild Minutes* is never mentioned again in the surviving letters.

The correspondence resumes with a December 22 letter from Lamantia, with which he sends the signed contract back with agreed-upon emendations. This is immediately followed by a detailed two-page letter dated December 25, accompanying the manuscript and largely consisting of notes on typographical minutiae. Notably, Philip decides against the quotation from the letter to Ginsberg that Ferlinghetti originally proposed including, preferring his later formulation, "I'm returning to my initial sources—like an act of nature," which appears on the back cover

---

8. *Golden Sardine* was printed photo-offset by Edwards Brothers in Ann Arbor, Michigan, according to Ralph T. Cook's *The City Lights Pocket Poet Series: A Descriptive Bibliography* (Laurence McGilvery/Atticus, 1982), p. 60.

of the final book. He ends this letter predicting the course of his subsequent poetic development:

> Last poem in book is I feel a real "seed" of what I hope to extend into—in fact, Secret Freedom [the third and final section title of *Selected Poems*], is altogether indicative of a newly found vein with its sources in the super-real...from deep inside & though I have other long poem, it didn't make it, for this selection,
> but feel soon much will roll out of mi black star!

This letter is followed by another dated December 26, confirming that he's sent the manuscript, which he sees as "DEFINITIVE[,]" though the overall selection of poems would undergo a minor amount of editorial wrangling. After confirming receipt of the manuscript and sending a $100 advance with a short note on January 3, 1967,[9] Ferlinghetti writes again on January 6, suggesting they cut three of the recent poems, "The Flying Fix," "Towers of the Rose Dawn," and "Capricorn Is a Wounded Knee," and add five from *Erotic Poems*, "Automatic World," "A Civil World," "Scenario," "Reality," and "A Simple Answer to the Enemy." Replying on January 17, Lamantia accedes to the cuts, but only approves the addition of "Automatic World" and "A Civil World." The others "would hang outside the *central mainline* as I've conceived it in the actual assemblage." On his part, Ferlinghetti responds on January 24 from Geneva, NY, en route to Europe, having changed his mind about "Towers" and "Capricorn," so only "The Flying Fix" ended up on the cutting-room floor.[10] There is also some discussion over the propriety of referring to William Blake as "Willie," but otherwise that's the extent of editorial back

---

9. Ferlinghetti's January 3 and 6 letters and Lamantia's January 17 reply are all mistakenly dated "1966," both poets writing the wrong year out of habit and muscle memory; the contents of these three letters confirm this, because they continue the discussion about *Selected Poems* from the December 1966 correspondence.

10. It appears in Lamantia's *Collected Poems* (p. 249).

and forth; the final book is little changed from the manuscript Philip and Nancy sent Lawrence from Spain on Christmas Day, 1966.

Published simultaneously with Kaufman's *Golden Sardine* in May 1967, the same month the Beatles release *Sgt. Pepper's Lonely Hearts Club Band*, Lamantia's *Selected Poems* appeared at a pivotal time for both Lamantia and City Lights. For Philip, *Selected Poems* essentially told the story of his relationship to surrealism in three chapters, from the breakthrough poems of his teenage years ("Revelations of a Young Surrealist"), to his period of estrangement from it ("Trance Ports"), to his triumphant return ("Secret Freedom"). Like *Touch of the Marvelous* from the previous year, *Selected Poems* was a chance to "correct the record," as it were, offering what he felt was a more suitable presentation of his poems than in their original book appearances. But unlike the former volume, which was a purely historical gathering of his teenage work, *Selected Poems* afforded him the opportunity to showcase both the poet that he had been and the poet he had become, and Lamantia's popular reputation doubtlessly owes much to the appearance of this compendium of his work in time for the Summer of Love.

At the same time, the book demonstrates Ferlinghetti's knack for evolving with the times, maintaining the cultural relevance of City Lights a good decade removed from the poetic revolution it had set in motion with the publication of Ginsberg's *Howl*. Though Lawrence's relationship to surrealism was ambivalent at best, he notably reached for it at the height of the psychedelic counterculture, sensing its fitness for the moment of hallucinogens and happenings, when Paul McCartney's collecting Magritte and nicking his apples for use as a record label. Ferlinghetti even savvily anticipates the popular resurgence of surrealism in France itself during the '68 general strike, and *Selected Poems* would sell some 5,000 copies in the first year; a second printing of 3,000 copies sold out by 1969, occasioning a third printing of 5,000 copies that City Lights sold over the next decade.[11] The book was even translated into French in 1996, under the title *Révélations d'un jeune surréaliste* (Éditions Jacques Brémond). Though *Selected Poems* was, in fact, "superseded" by City Lights' publication of an updated "New and Selected Poems" called *Bed of Sphinxes* (1997), given the availability now of all of Lamantia's work in his *Collected Poems*, we've decided to republish the earlier book due to its greater significance to the history of City Lights and the Pocket Poets Series.

---

11. These figures appear in Cook's *Bibliography* (p. 58) and are consistent with a notation on the book's file in the office at City Lights.

Philip Lamantia, passport photo, ca. 1962

Lawrence Ferlinghetti to Philip Lamantia, August 26, 1966

CITY LIGHTS BOOKS
261 COLUMBUS AVENUE, SAN FRANCISCO 11

26 Aug 66

Dear Phillip:
Allen showed me yr letter & I am eager to do a
book of yours.(It's about time! What?)
What about SELECTED POEMS OF PHILLIP LAMANTIA
or wd you prefer something wilder & more
beautiful? I wd quote yr letter to Allen in a
little note at the beginning: ""I believe, more
than ever, that there is something else, and that
It is within us, your Flower, my Fire, Blake's
Genius, the ka of Egypt, the One Thing of Trismegis-
tus...and it can be transmitted & survive in the
Great Return to the Source...................
....God, of course, does not exist-- the Unique is,
though, we continue...." (I have made a copy of
this page of yr letter/hope you don't mind.)
Call the book THE POETIC TRANCE?--from yr phrase in
letter "The Poetic Trance for me is the place of
locating" ???? Of course, I wouldn't use any
of this unless you dug....It's yr book, you make
it, I'll print it, I mean publish it.....So yr
bk cud be "new work" or collected "old" work....
Let me hear....
I am tranced to see you walking thru Malaga again
these days. If you ever go out to Nerja again,
please give Angelina our love and kiss.....We think
of her and her grave man often (Celestino) and the
children too.....I hope they will not be eaten up
by Franco & tourism. (When Nerja comes to Torre-
molino, so endeth the world)....

dreamer---- *lawrence*

LF

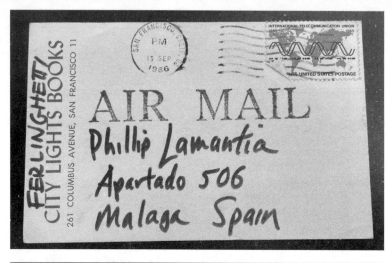

Lawrence Ferlinghetti to Philip Lamantia, September 3, 1966

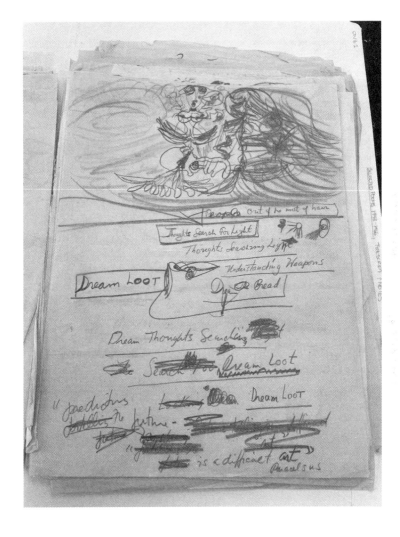

Philip Lamantia, "Dream Loot," ca. November 1966

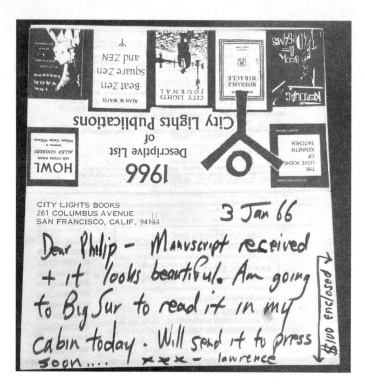

Lawrence Ferlinghetti to Philip Lamantia, January 3, 196[7]

Long galleys from Villiers Publications, London, ca. March 1967

Note the author. Galley proofs of the
original set but not here were clean.

—JES

With

Compliments

VILLIERS PUBLICATIONS LTD
Ingestre Road
Tufnell Park
London NW5
(01) 485 9404 (2 lines)

with my wings aglitening in the night
and about words heard tomorrow
in a little peasant cart
of the seventeenth century

Breath by breath
the vase in the tomb
breaks to give birth to a roving Sphinx
Trouble, sweet bird, sweet lion
hunger for you
hunger for your mother

The children in the lamps
play with our hair
swinging over the void

Here is a landscape on fire
Here are horses wet by the sour fluids of women

On the pillars of nicotine
the word pleasure is erased by a dog's tongue
On the pillars the bodies are opened by keys
the keys are nailed to my belt
to be touched at dawn
to be used in a dream

If our name sound is heard
the children will come to murder
at the bottom of the lake
at the bottom of the lake

If the children murder
the owls will bleed
the wanton humans
who parade in halucinations of the sun

When the countries fall into the sea
with a crash involving prophecies and madmen
together in a little cradle
lifted into the robes of desire
and with our mouths opened for the stars
howling for the castles to melt at our feet
you and I
will ride over the breasts of our mother
who knows no one
who was born from unknown birds
forever in silence
forever in dreams
forever in the sweat of fire

YOU AND I HAVE NOTHING TO FEAR

Listen
you may hear the ten may poles
out of a womb
pulled through the child's stupefying algebra
of sound
but only if you dip bracelets
in your blood
scratch out the eyes set in my ruby
that is
in turn
set in the sun
washed and preserved
for the toys of unity

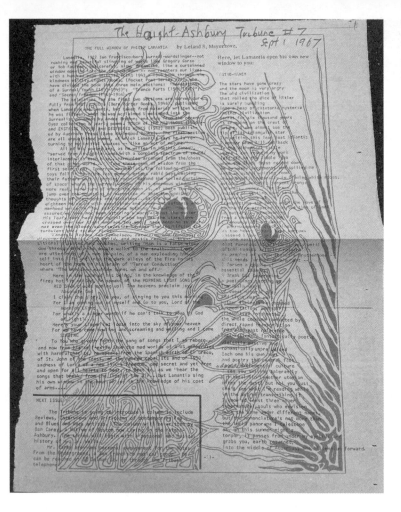

Review of *Selected Poems* in *The Haight-Ashbury Tribune*, September 1, 1967

Lawrence Ferlinghetti to Philip Lamantia, September 3, 1966